FLIRT FORMULA

ANNE PORTUGAL

Flirt Formula

TRANSLATION
BY
Jean-Jacques Poucel

La Presse
IOWA CITY & PARIS 2012

Published in the United States by La Presse,
an imprint of Fence Books

La Presse/Fence Books are distributed by Consortium
www.cbsd.com
www.lapressepoetry.com

Library of Congress Control Number 2012931613
Portugal, Anne
Flirt Formula by Anne Portugal,
translated by Jean-Jacques Poucel
p. cm.

ISBN 9781934200537

1. French poetry. 2. Poetry. 3. Contemporary translation.

First Edition
10 9 8 7 6 5 4 3 2 1

FLIRT FORMULA

we loved to surrender barely located know
that we were naïve
just juxtaposed bouquets
that each of us had a social hook
minimum tender

of the fancy surprise we would say
secret contact
of the bonds of the flow
we were precisely
speaking line
just so from order to another

The simple exercise to his beloved
to his newest the earthly dwelling
cannot ring white lily triumphant
where to put him address misplaces
all bodies nearby

having seen one's own being inside
a format she was so let's do it again
within a globe more than the first
in the filaments his being born
held over for once more.

Dear only decor it must be small
welcome opacity model it shadow it
with strokes pauses the feel
for another you I love to hold
pin prick in the light insect blood

bonus shrunk edifice the needle
so now in the competition
of wings at will it will flit about
spit nails bang into the set
is offered sharp in alfa precision.

This overture called an origin
on a wide-open road section
dust to the evil halt good captain
simple consolidation of banisters
adept to await the fairy as low as
you and her however she embroiders

gentle surfaces to change start at go
her olden days all silvery suspicious
that park excludes that on the pass
rarely meets them panorama dear friends
a crowd of people your buttons dot embodies
cartoon delivery bores her decorates lanes.

His entire morning cringes umlaut his
slimness each time forever is mentioned
evidently select cypress its minute value
a graphic character dreams of it
in crowds an imitating regent

prior prelude prior to his birth he is there prior
to him wrote it with the other from orleans in mind
all travel expenses ice cubes and the list is done
for he who wants to be kidnapped we are the experts
or claim to be willingly.

Va frère to reach the town initials roses
to your name paint lips on fair miller-maid
an index of you simply conditional
can't condense this role give and take
opium motion process a producer's log
and the matter would the very fairest be

porsche the neck rushing course in veins
improved saw the sun until stopped just in front
spent red volume radical reform discussed
thought a bit that all is residency instead
of grass it's a pursing of the lips individuals
beautiful pointy dolphins going home.

Freely travelling with everything but the kitchen sink
ever so pleased all was happening eccentrically
in his favor dwelling in between in mixed company
and trailing calmer she too preferred appear
and disappear with a gute nacht going
on the topic saying to herself service belongs
to the immediate

right one health in isolation the good flow
of the river a first name with landscapes helping
himself with these little clues and so what's next
the sidekick catalogue permits him to follow along
situate good night without a consequence
taking place underneath and how do you do
his ready set go.

Of perpetual effort spared just from void
rallied her early into his library and she
had the keys drove around the long afternoons
on the water was to be example
drew up circles clearly appeared just in front
turned humane sectioned the putting into place

himself surprised would not further rev it
in tune his body geared surrendered to the flow
he grants it adopting do you expect to find a fine
burrow so fresh a succession of white
all lined up on some plain his exerting
radical he invented how he was belonging.

Perfect there will be speed
a sliver of sky the fixer
causes an end puts a period
to the manic articulations
naked segments so far gone

chubby sky were we to harvest
gold leaves would require such apt things
as lie in ambush an adult aspect
gently fitting in triumph to ensure
folded we it unfolding.

Were he to be included the secret agent
apparent seen on the bench and the house glides
pleases him to what good end cannot be
made to wait hello Sunday couple seeing
as he would detail finish the war

bear the slight having left his bench
entirely plain concert the illusion just as well outside
that love as soon as the song was recording not far
from the woods the air the lawn shared and the rain
a private pencil recalling a proportion.

Starts up a welling in an extraordinary vehicle
generalizing the colors he braces against the forces
of corruption the draw of a nightingale's lesson
on the nice billboards hubba hubba
he motors meets her by the church
he explains refocused effort it's me
I'm your turbo diesel

spares her zone of discoloring under impression
hand held creature to which a valve
attended grafted knots a scale's edges the tourniquet
one who does not at this instant see you who has not had
my heart through arias decides he does not want it
he'd bind her in a manner of incursion at a balcony
she and it's studied overexposes in repetition.

On the dance floor whose
color ravishing to the memory
what exists with butterflies
what were you called
girl said marie
spirit of
already too complicated

green thus often I shall dream
have the slight feeling that was
little pyramid acts
speaks more of minutiae
stability galaxy
the natural consequence
in this we are friends.

Absolutely pleased fully sincere
agreeing in his path the broadening
succeeding sidewalk became place
of human existence a sample
on paper exchanged with his wild friend

up against existence he was lifted is model
on a canapé touches dew a fresh setting
of no project that could obtain
gesture for a stupefying overstep
that shall never body be.

Fact animals rush best the departure
décor me I like foxes a muzzle the horn is black
sofa enclosure his preference for the motif were I alone
may as well play back the made to scale
symphony of band-aids

two sharing a hershey's kiss works every time
setting fire to and the story sees the time has come
the end of the fields the road the little enticements
fatally the interior the fancy between two people
engaged in keeping it simple.

One of the two a character had he been sent
his existing copy a sub-fife his brother
doorstep offensive the ftd florist of wheat
to see him melody contestant so ta-da the young
folk full of novelties life lets them
jump all excited the glint of small privateers

another of whom a young body his friend with a collection
it's in the album restitution of the botanical garden
commands marchons marchons in eminent general's style
by this that makes him modern visible in the light
he shows himself in closeup he who was running easy
to make it all too sharp won't you sometimes close your eyes.

Your wish of you
condition of nobody
you pass by all the princes
each of whom
on the beach interrupted
communicates

bon appétit of course
before the by passing
your arctic tendency
gratifies bursts of shadows
will have slipped the ferret
into the mystery choice.

Directions as if cancelled the place
in flight but not just on paper benefits
of a sport he received requires assent
an envelop received form the service
a high conduct line symmetrically free
his fall a calculated imperfection
just a spot pulp right under palm trees

a spirit sensitive to matter moves
its episodes make it bigger no trace
of the big reverberations the number two
fills the fear stretches a plank
a single string on the theory of conflicts
joy the game power four
as dangerous as possible.

He will blossom under commands
blond in line container to point to
his face on the rest of the world
projectile indicating saints the other
in gold slays him the interval the lambs
the closer to the grass you are

get a handle get a grip a roller
coaster zip-a-dee-doo-dah gang
sport for our wings and crossing the projection
we of stones knocking them out everyone
who wanted to establish obsession
had blacked-out turned to the walls.

Featherstone place agreed
feather and stone
sound of bloom
jacket of air
manœuvre of heart
the all median
luxury leather handling
interior of joy

how jane speaks
about her life
stream two enjoined
a bit brothers
the index opposing
especially seen against
the rose tint
recaresses remarkably calm.

Imagine deepening the impression
of green not entirely it's flashy not too
touching its constructs you develop
well-meant manœuvres a gusto
surrendered to the morning partner club
by his side of death in the clear just to see

that ideas are simple their tiny vision
of confection will you have one egg or two
make me rather a good tinkerbell helper
a producer of clarity who featured to sift so
in the end by consent the dawn of the take
could be of grass but also your departure.

How not to think from this
meadow comes sheer frankness
the familial group the ball it
is from it it is coming
the liaison agent double
frame saga sets two windows

the model age of the achieved plant
with but a few tweaks can be quick
off the blocks in self confidence
and the choir when it hits select
all holds the gathering upright
summer and now a definite position.

Namely in the air
we would be becoming this invisible
water set its map the context
the real limits would be continuing
probably the world on its way

everything accrues happy together clicks
continues resembles the chronology of the other
mechanically organizes
as its form
in other words our life.

Ring dancing makes us one the right talk in tropes
turns upon very lively red and its resolution
you should be queen go visit weird people
and our acts squared shoulder on one small plate
are stretched out and the arm that came to your help
childhoods here the up-side-down team

such reproach at it is leveled at the baby chariot
there airs huff puff for miles what is
blended that in this we could way on up there
upon prairies placing the day its opposite corner
ourselves mingle all the heft the quality so
now look we are in your camp.

Own the zone bring your accessories back
from now on this surprising principle
this little army that with us he is discovering
are you not handsomely fond of the prologue
floors it the pedal to its salvation
overture's program one in which heroes

holding the intervals external
spontaneously ring dancing does us all good does
us thus is going to do and to boot we gaze at each other
includes the idea of a bridge in its making it appears
credit but one in the service of luck
here we are under the map we are waving.

Let's meditate landscape what all
our powers do arms around the neck
simple visit and suspend
without difficulty ancient horse
we distinguish our demeanor

summer without others that distinction
goes entirely hazy with
the habitual cutting down of hedgerows
and yet the starlet tree in the group what he has
resolved on his account we too.

Some observed not lived animals
flung opposing them
to the deficit in our moods of the sort
that puts their deformations to use
preoccupied just singing

in our on one level nature
its duration did not mean a thing
we played mountain airs
marginal notes for dragons we
the guardian all the while goose bumps.

Aiming the change of a whole body
caretaking of everyone in the service of your closest
on the recliner just now leaning
you got the feeling flat screen dear friends
the great service to go is in the manner
that he cries wails just now see you
his prism service his wuthering

in front of a jack rabbit dish prompt the road
where he went walking surprise glass or gun shot
he negotiates engaged in bearing in mind that
retying life that very day the trumpet and what follows
risk running hot seated not far puffing
heightens the sound trumpets the sound gives
redness darkness in that place.

In the swinging where sand is thrown her life passed
she too on the simply abstained balcony
thickness at the window imagines the wolf
well distinguished future comes wonder happens
like the normal coming to the rescue of being

in the cordial manor if you must send the solo
here's the new grid youth the silverware
some great art in whichever forests the wolf
whom you just drafted the elite force
had been enlisted in your patents.

Were you to take the vasco voyage gama boat
slightly overboard you copy the requested
lines no possible reconstitution
neither the size nor the anchor a spin
on the same circuit a warning lounge
for which the drifting trace it draws out
by selected measure is yet to be assembled

where a watermill a little industrial center
better supplied by a clock
when you lean in on it filed under transport
and stories to boot
the construction is what follows
the paddle excelling at detachment
merges to a dash deck-planks to modify.

To render mobility that can in reality
outside duration
not feel the sunshine from there he engages
the last mohican
who come to think of him sees himself shown
the lighting turned on

window simple on the camp the sky
associated thanks to a map
recourse to the genre enjoys awaiting
watchword
and windless carnations the last
in adding regrets.

To the west a remaining stand
is giving its real place back
weakened domino
escaped by putting everything far away
it unpacks a prairie house
a guy from the last century
water lukewarm moderate thrill
had spent days at court

the space between two wallpapers
where flowers soak
the unprepared rains the birch trees
two for every castle
a bedroom is a precise place
feeds its fire plays copy on its sheep
of a common feature it projects
which is what it consists of.

Inverse inverse but french in saying it
in discovering they were speaking rays
they would remain separate therein
an expeditious equivocal
ahem idea of their being
beams powerful blanks nonetheless
basta not a word their lives

a swan regime recounted generic
paddling the center of the basin
that along the line to the polar detriment
we descend normally rejuvenated
we play it mercy in the directive life
sincerity little trigger boredom
designated in its appearance.

Regulate adoration jewel feathers
service to men the connoisseur
moderate release a postcard
in cut up matter

add on intense stupor neon
into his hand to fold the subject envelop
for her set down was talking no doubt
of a dog-eared corner.

Fantasized ruled out does it not come over
the lorelei model click all headlights out
it will flash calculus a screen later
the maiden box apprentices will go diving in
against the flow at its execution

voice in headphones you will open up best friend
needle pines parthenopa to consecrated objects
imagining prior to illusions thinner and thinner
that we'd made small talk got used to it darling
never confirmed hymn fait accompli.

Skeletons for programming
everyone a thousand sands
indeed we recognize such a body
tenured says that it goes forward
takes off in a neighboring subject
the last rain getting carried away
will not repair the step
downstroke

he who was living
import export hyper predictable
in good exact and dramatic health
brings the heart of this topic to life
his empire eclipsed body
in the frog in his flask
that allows for lighting
by filtration.

The quality series forcibly a difficult bit
is not so insistent is not there
to underline to stress the gray
anonymity apart everything's
warehouse competes owned a stone
trained coincides is led from the inside

once again the era gratified
less enchanted by causes
the slightest overlap earlier ones
previously known affair relieves
in the fashion of attachment
the effort equal to its distribution.

In amusing was the essential vector
common white by badge the
little doctor he tells him minima
he tells him in saying so what it is and
you knew had certainly contributed

that in the future will yield
retribution that first existence
that's why to speak from now on
with them in the filaments raised
we water only in the morning.

Slowly flakes aggress his anger
glasses of water
the compliments made to him
fire-screen teensy sisters terrain harvests
sticks to his ribs fruits to marble
inclusion in the quartz promised
to game cocktail wild thoughts

a corporation is founded
in the articulation of the white lamps
stretched symmetry pulley
in short the one and onlys
who have effectively delay repeated folds reflexes
the buck axis blurs parked
the disposition of the buck's hooves.

The compensation hydra phase
the trusted clean path day entitled
integrity transition modesty
sentimentality off the coast of
our rest to hear you say it
then retire on an expedition

a breathing guide the other them
of base definition the figure to depart
is the neighborhood is a fake
is not at home projected remakes
himself to the register of the fixed
establishments.

Last act modern conversation
quite the tone becoming one
model to the first the cruiser he knows
is underway several will have translated
tight negligee the saintly dialogue
the elasticity announcement whose function
is to free this play of legs

bebop a slug's style
private edge on verge legs too
except that black and the duration of the loan
the cozy mandala the spots that play
the intellect in the caboose
I have a beloved not far from here
a superior budget.

Immensity as manner of intervening
concerted bit tongue sticking out
hooray at whom shall we now play
happy as one who separates a lark
attaching it to the edge of the landscape
by documentation of the instant

medium swing the dramatic penchant
of situating a loved one the invariant
splitting up of regionalist jobs
style of laughter target on the flower
patterned carpet voilà the fan is back
moved by the big time.

A lane whose degree frames it
nap left him inside
is a preparation to impress
relative diminishes
the new translation of
had I the air of

a tiny cross and a pencil
but also your cheetah
weakness
precarious imperfect
narrow difference of sorrow
place name names it.

He who by shoulder went
worry free in lanes nor branchia
the breath
that steers
the waters lesson
was film paper with his childhood

from the heart from the macabre
his wife
escapes
actualizes the turn
continues doubles up touches at last
and in deepening in name is desperation.

It didn't make our entire trip
that clinical analysis of the world
what of the bowdlerized fetid knight
an idyll that concerns you
a distinction for the high seas
when it's missing prior to fiction

says the king the commerce of crisis
would deploy banners to the company
the following body map is a good object
perfect talking let's make sure that it
remain on the screen it will fold make due
a community clinic in the alignment.

It seizes him from a single city so
how about we play pilot standard
motor jack in whom my words bob
for it's for a shepherd's song
his place on the watchtower romances
the patterns he squares in sidecar
accomplice via elimination

he needs a definition of the domain
a bonus monument disguised
that's all the howls as rubato
scams played sold balls to the wall
they as if to say were helping him bind
and the big subscription real life
thunderstruck them to look to the ground.

Formula Flirts

Tous les gestes de notre vie étaient assortis d'un vers.

According to Anne Portugal, *Flirt Formula,* the fifth of her nine book-length poems to be translated into English, represents, poetically speaking, "the sum of all my sins," even if her declared intention was also to write "a very light book," a poem that would "sit like a bird on a branch," "amount to next to nothing."

In a sense, when she speaks about her poetry, when she speaks in poems, every turn of phrase Portugal uses has the potential to become a formula, every cluster of words, ingredients enlisted in a method she is inventing to achieve something specific (quite often something as of yet unnamed because as of yet unknown).

Yet, if hidden desires are generative forces in *Flirt Formula* — and one would be well-advised in guessing so — it is telling that in interviews Portugal does not directly speak of attraction, of fantasy, and of seduction, but rather attributes the overarching impulses in flirtation to modalities of restraint: "the crux of poetry is the art of not touching it."

At a moment when other French and Francophone poets are actively inscribing personal identity into politically motivated forms, anchoring their meaning making processes deep into the inner workings of project poems, Portugal undertakes an entirely different set of risks, some of them still attached to what may, in the current context, be considered antiquated versions of poetry, all of them invested in the strategic displacement of meaning in verse: "I wanted to do the opposite, to make something that would be like a glancing, that would also be that very way meaning has of settling into lines of verse without however being perceptible; that is, the idea of a 'flirtation' is still the idea of an avoidance."

In her paratextual remarks, the metaphor Portugal recursively uses to explain the set up of *Flirt Formula* hinges on the introduction of a single named figure, a central persona who enacts, if only once, the dramatic constitution of subjectivity, a purely grammatical affair in this book, as indeed it is in her previous writings: "There is a character who appears just once, the character of Jane from *Tarzan*."

Undoubtedly this choice of figure implies primal urges, the bodacious nudity that springs to mind based on Edgar Rice Burroughs' books, or their screen and comic book adaptations. And, casting Jane and Tarzan in flirt scenarios might well prompt the rehearsal of such communicative difficulties as beset those newly love-struck, especially those complexities facing couples for whom there is a language barrier. But these are not the traits Portugal explicitly underlines in "how jane speaks" (43).

Rather, it is the athletic ability associated with this intertextual figure that helps Portugal establish the conceptual rigging for the hermeneutic code at play in her poem; in the figure of Jane she identifies a swinger, one who leaps into the void of a sentence, grabs onto a vine of syntax, and swings through a jungle of meaning: "In truth, what amused me was precisely adopting [Jane's] position in relation to the text: that is, you leap, you grab a vine, you swing, and thus you think you've accomplished the poetic gesture, only to find that it must be replayed."

If this meaning game seems tailor-made for the trapeze artist reader, one who delights in launching into each new sentence in an adventurous spirit of discovery, its mechanisms are predicated on some of Portugal's greatest poetic predilections — her so-called "sins" — namely, her weakness for poems that, in the self-same gesture, theorize their very ground of becoming, attempt to realize those terms, and, in imitation of nineteenth century models, allow for failure to be a full measure of success: "It scares me, moreover, really scares me because, basically, there's an old school aspect to the project; that is, the idea of replaying an old-fashioned notion of poetry, right at the moment when absolutely everything [traditional] is being abandoned."

Flirting with failure in this context is not merely an enticement into self-destructive release (see "the lorelei model" [72]). Rather, the risk taking, however sincere its approval of naïveté, however extreme its allowance of difficulty, is uncompromisingly underwriting conditions for permanent renewal: "In fact, it's a small pleasure to which I've treated myself, with all the dangers it entails."

In the degree to which these perpetual first encounters do lead to a story of great love, one that unfolds over the course of the poem—and Portugal's ambition in this is unmitigated—its greatness is sustained through an expansive, a disciplined, love of language in all of its formalities, beginning and ending with the possibilities of the single sentence, of which there are exactly forty-four in *Flirt Formula*, each set into motion, according to the codes of its typographical setting.

In other words, the opening line—think of it as an icebreaker—is the principal technique in *Flirt Formula*. Portugal's *"phrase d'attaque"* undauntedly recalls both Mallarmé and Ronsard in its compressed, accelerated parataxis. Half blackmailed come-on, half abstracted renunciation (the rather rare kind that wins the day by surrender), each first line is also the last line, is already all middle, and, stretching from the capital letter of the first word on the top left to the full stop on the bottom right of the facing page, it characteristically swerves in register from popular diction to diction that verges on the precious, the noble, the awkwardly self-discovering.

The facing-page stanzas, in other words, while distinct typographically, are intertwined and act as if they were one and the same body: constituted of desiring words, they work with, against, and on each other; they are in constant conversation, very much as if each stanza were a condensed corporeal emanation resulting from the flirting couple's discourse.

If in most cases there is some independent coherence in grammatical unity at the level of the stanza, the line of verse and the syntactical clause do not necessarily coincide (as they would in traditional French prosody), thereby keeping the way in which words can recombine very much up in the air. How to punctuate the main sentence, how to prioritize or subordinate clauses, which words to read as if off-set by imaginary dashes or commas, all of this remains open-ended, in flux, tasks for the reader to determine.

The metaphor of vine swinging comes in handy to explain how this all works: at times, small word clusters may appear dense, heavy with g-forces when, at the lowest point in the arc of their swing, compact in the velocity of the curve, the production of even loosely fitting meaning requires a firm grip on the part of the reader who, like the grammatical personae inhabiting the poems, circulates by bobbing up and down through the jungle of signs; at times, other word clusters may appear as weightless as when, at the apogee of their upward trajectory, they momentarily stall, as if suspended, afloat for an ephemeral second in the melody of the sentence. Portugal evokes this tension between the mass and the weightlessness of words, again, as one of her particular pleasures in writing: "What I especially like is to impose a principle of lightness on words that sometimes weigh a ton."

To achieve this principle of lightness, Portugal injects a steady flow of airiness and levity into the joints of the sentence, often simply by eliminating what normally joins syntax together (conjunctions, prepositions, articles, punctuation). Consequently, in *Flirt Formula* the elements of story telling, synecdoche, metaphor, and allegory all remain just partially present in the "manic articulations" (22), each participating in building the duo's meditative contra-facing postures, but each also ultimately truncated, telegraphed by the fast thinking, the glancing by, the target missing.

Here too, the near miss, the trajectories that barely touch are not quite inconsequential. They produce a peculiar kind of distinction. In the snatches of words, however fragmented, there is often a core distillation of gestures, distinct in themselves, though run together over the course of time, minutely intertwined and traversing one another along the obstacle course of the sentence. These "tiny vision[s] of confection" (45) enjoy such distinction as can be made by a visual image (especially partial), by a song clip (even if distantly implied), by the precise character of a passing phrase reused just so, at a precise moment, in the midst of an initial conversation, along the way on a road trip, inside the desperate whispers of a blistering love affair, each made into a moment textually by the disposition of sensations that memorably creates them in exactly that way.

How then do you locate what's weightless in this poem? How are its networks of vines illuminated? The principle of levity is animated by multiplicity. On the one hand, temporality in the poems is most often plural, intersecting the imperative mood with the present, the past perfect tense with the past imperfect; seduction, recollection, and loss seamlessly inhabit the same breath. On the other hand, there are multiple ways to string meaning together between the poems printed in vis-à-vis.

Portugal has stated that the "swinging" can be imagined as contra-sensual, where the implied subjects — the *he* and *she*, the *I* and *you*, often implied by way of carefully placed possessive adjectives — swing in opposite directions, crossing and swapping places somewhere in the middle of the sentence. These orchestrated chassées-croisés establish an immediately apparent echo-network, a constellation of call and responses between the "*juxtaposed bouquets*" (7): where the left-hand poem speaks of a "small décor," the right-hand poem speaks of a "shrunk edifice," of a "set" made "in alfa precision" (10-11).

Such corresponding associations in the lexical field accrue through recursive variation and repetition ("she overexposes in repetition" [27]), and it is as if the act of missing each other, the glancing right by one another, were rooted in saying the same things differently, or saying different things with similar words. In addition, the fact of missing one another is already inscribed, as the opening poem states, in the very condition of apostrophe: the "simple exercise" of speech "cannot ring white lily triumphant" because "address misplaces" the potential beloved (8).

Alternately, the "swinging" can be imagined as consensual, where the implied subjects may cling to the same vine, or different vines, leaping more or less at the same time, more or less in the same direction, arriving more or less at the same place, and so on. In speaking about how this style of reading works in her poem, Portugal uses the French expression meaning "to go away on an extended weekend" (*faire le pont*), but the lover's leap to which she refers — "the idea of a bridge in its making" (53) — is the acrobatic leap the reader can make from one poem to the next, such that the first line on the left is followed by the fist line on the right, and so on, down the page. Consider for example, the extended top line on pages 44 and 45: "Imagine deepening the impression // that ideas are simple their tiny vision // of green..."

Spanning the gutter in this fashion works only for some poems in the French; I have attempted to allow for it to work in some poems in the English. Since Portugal is consciously reworking traditional poetic forms, it is useful to remark that this re-introduction of a caesura in this bridge or leaping line recalls the balanced hemistiches of traditional French verse form. In addition, jumping over the fold of the book in this manner, casting the space of the poem over two face-to-face pages recalls the basic set up of Mallarmé's *Un coup de dés*, though in Portugal's work, the visual clusters of words have blended back into deceptively normative looking stanzas.

There are in fact many invisible games at work in *Flirt Formula*, some of which pose insurmountable challenges to a translator. During the translation process, a particularly salient example came to light while speaking with Portugal about the poem beginning "Fantasized ruled out" (72-73).

The problem has to do with a sound game she is playing in the French, a game that is briefly described elsewhere in the poem—"Inverse inverse but french in saying it" (68)—and that only a very careful, carefree reader of French might catch onto. Here, for the sake of explanation is the stanza in question:

> *voix dans le casque meilleur ami vous ouvrirez*
> *pins d'aiguilles parthénope aux consacrés objets*
> *envisager d'avant minces plus en plus d'illusions*
> *qu'on puisse meubler s'est habitué chéri*
> *n'a jamais confirmé hymne fait accompli.*

The poem itself contains two famous figures of jilted love, Lorelei and Parthenope (Jane does indeed have good company in *Flirt Formula*). Thus, being a poem about rebuff and consequential suicides, its meanings are particularly dense and especially difficult to decode in this second stanza. What Anne quickly pointed out to me in passing is that the last segment of the poem was made to be reversible, almost the way we used to play vinyl records backwards.

That is, "hymne fait accompli" (which I've opted to keep in the English) can be read backward, as "pli qu'on a fait hymne" (fold we made into a hymn). An alternate transcription of this stanza, one that differs from the one found on page 73, might attempt to present these lines in their opposite direction, to present the "Inverse in verse" but in English, which might look something like this:

the fold we made into a hymn and never confirmed
dear, got used, got cherished, to decorate, since we
slimmer and slimmer illusions from before were imagining
the consecrated objects — parthenope — needles of pines
open will you, friend, in the helmet voices.

For readers familiar with Portugal's work, such acrobatic syntax is not too surprising: the traces of reversible parataxis are visible in some of her earlier writing (for example in a poem in which the verbs "passes" and "gives" alternate [see *Nude* p. 35], a poem that has been set to music by Rodolphe Burger). In this case, however, it is difficult not to wonder if the reversibility is not there to add another allusive fold to this already richly intertextual poem, namely a gestural reference to the poem "Reversibility" by Baudelaire.

The principal difficulties of translating *Flirt Formula*, present at every turn, are nearly always associated with rendering the precise lightness of each phrase. There is something singularly cool about the tone of Anne's sentences, a unique liveliness that immediately strikes you, though its techniques are hard to perceive. In an attempt to translate the hues of her cool tones, I have, at times, taken quite a bit of liberty, mostly encouraged by the author who was exceptionally generous with her time throughout the process. In many cases, what came to light was that word for word translations were the clunkiest possible solution, and the further away I moved from these, the lighter the solutions became. The classic case in point, one to illustrate what I mean, is none other than the flirt formula itself, the sole phrase to appear on the back of the book:

Vers un métier fraîcheur avec une chute.

The simplest, most direct rendering of this signature phrase would probably be the first of the five solutions listed below. Yet the one I've chosen is rather far removed from it, and I could be guilty here, as well as throughout, of preferring solutions motivated by my own invisible desires:

Toward a freshness vocation with a fall.

To a practice in levity and its downfall.

Approaching a cheekiness vocation with rebuff.

By craft of charm and a let down.

Of a cool living with a drop.

Within the realm of making meaning, the imminent dangers of flirtation keep us vacillating between being misunderstood or too well understood. This is what poetry can teach us: how to walk the thin line between remaining desirable (precisely by what is left unsaid) and risking rejection (for wanting too much, or for being found wanting).

When reading *Flirt Formula,* think of the mechanics of movement in hot and happening couples dancing, the way energy coils tight in the dancers' bodies, releases, extends, bounces back, keeps moving along the elasticity of multiple, united but diverting, lines of action, driven onward partly by the pulse of the music, partly by sheer attraction, and the panoply of eschewals that ensues. The greater the tug on the habits of reference, on the worn out habit of sensation, the more illuminated are words and things, what we make of them, within their dynamic contingencies.

Jean-Jacques Poucel

OTHER BOOKS BY THE AUTHOR

Les commodités d'une banquette
P.O.L, Paris, 1983

De quoi faire un mur
P.O.L, Paris, 1978

Le plus simple appareil
P.O.L, Paris 1992

Fichier
Michel Chandeigne, Paris, 1992

Dans la reproduction en 2 parties égales des plantes et des animaux, with Suzanne Doppelt
P.O.L, Paris, 1999

Voyer en l'air
Editions de l'Attente, Bordeaux, France, 2001

définitif bob
P.O.L, Paris, 2002

et le gens contents de se baigner
Editions de l'Attente, Bordeaux, France, 2009

la formule flirt
P.O.L, Paris, 2010

BOOKS TRANSLATED BY THE AUTHOR

Paramour, by Stacy Doris
Translation, with Caroline Dubois
P.O.L, Paris, 2009

BOOKS BY THE AUTHOR
IN ENGLISH TRANSLATION

Nude, translated by Norma Cole
Kelsey Street Press, Berkeley, California, 2001

Quisite moment, translated by Rosmarie Waldrop
Burning Deck Press, Providence, Rhode Island, 2007

and people happy to go swimming, translated by Jean-Jacques Poucel
in *POEM*, Fishdrum, 2009

absolute bob, translated by Jennifer Moxley,
Buring Deck Press, Providence, Rhode Island, 2010

ABOUT THE AUTHOR

Born in Angers, France, Anne Portugal is a poet and a translator. She lives in Paris where she teaches French, contemporary literature and writing, as well as the occasional course in rhetoric to students of advertising. She has published widely in journals and anthologies and has collaborated with artists, art museums, and the radio program France-Culture. With Abigail Lang and Vincent Broqua, she is currently translating Caroline Bervall's *Meddle English.*

ABOUT THE TRANSLATOR

A native of Denver, Colorado, Jean-Jacques Poucel is a poet, translator, and professor of French literature at the University of Calgary. He has written about the experimental poetics of the Oulipo, including *Jacques Roubaud and the Invention of Memory*. He is currently translating Emmanuel Hocquard's *Une Grammaire de Tanger*.

After they met in 2008, Jean-Jacques Poucel and Anne Portugal collaborated on a short poem entitled "Procedural symmetry" (forthcoming in *READ*, Tamaas & 1913).

This is the ninth title in the La Presse series
of contemporary French poetry in translation.
The series is edited by Cole Swensen,
and designed by Shari DeGraw.
Flirt Formula is typeset in
Adobe Jenson.